ABOVE: *This farmstead, though probably no more than fifty years old, shows the Hanoverian tradition of the central yard with buildings round it, as well as mock-Tudor timbering.*

COVER: *The thirteenth-century barn at Great Coxwell in Oxfordshire (National Trust).*

OLD FARM BUILDINGS

Nigel Harvey
M.A., A.R.I.C.S.

Shire Publications Ltd.

CONTENTS

Printed in Great Britain by C. I. Thomas &
Sons (Haverfordwest) Ltd, Press Buildings,
Merlins Bridge, Haverfordwest.

British Library Cataloguing in Publication Data available.

PQ

02431652

One of the last of the traditional farm cider-presses, once common in the West Country. The circular
building which housed such presses was known as the 'pound house' from the action of the press.

A haybarn near Wensleydale. A surveyor in 1800 described this area as 'remarkable for its haybarns, which are situated on the centre of every third or fourth field. They always have a cowhouse at one end, and frequently at both, where the cattle are wintered. By this arrangement, the hay and manure are not carried any great distance, an important circumstance in these hilly countries.'

THE LEGACY OF THE PAST

Old farm buildings are among the most attractive relics of our rural past. They are also among the most interesting, for in their various ways they tell us much about the life and work of our farming ancestors.

For one thing, they preserve the imprint of the farming systems and tools for which they were designed. For example, the barn recalls the flailers who so laboriously thrashed the corn-harvest in the long winter months. For another, they illustrate the building materials and methods of their time. In particular, they show the dependence of builders in the days before the factory and the railway on the local materials of their areas, on Devon cob, on Cotswold limestone, on Midland clay, brick and thatch, on Welsh slate and on York-shire millstone grit. Then, too, they record the changing fortunes and techniques of agriculture down the generations, since many of the old buildings which now survive have been adapted to new purposes. Stables, for example, have sometimes become milking parlours, while eighteenth century barns have been adapted to a variety of twentieth century uses. Each farm building has its own particular story to tell. So has each farmstead, the central group of buildings which forms the farmer's indoor workshop.

This book seeks to increase the reader's understanding of his rural heritage by enabling him to learn more of it for himself from the farm buildings that he sees around him when he walks or drives in the countryside.

ABOVE: *The 14th-century tithe barn at Bradford-on-Avon, Wiltshire, is one of the finest of the magnificent buildings erected by wealthy ecclesiastical landowners for storing and thrashing corn, including corn paid as a form of rent. This one was built of stone with buttresses to prevent the walls splaying outwards under the weight of the roof.*

BELOW: *The interior of a late medieval tithe barn in Middlesex. It uses the framed system of construction in which upright posts support roof members to form aisled structures. This made possible considerably larger buildings than the more primitive 'cruck' system.*

Thrashing by flail in the late 18th century. Corn is stored either in the barn or in ricks in the nearby stackyard. The ricks stand on staddle-stones to protect them from rats and mice. The staddles, like the barn, are built of local stone. A cloth is rigged across the entrance of the barn to prevent the entry of poultry.

THE BARN

The barn remains one of the most obvious and familiar of all farm buildings. Historically, indeed, it dominated many farmsteads from the Middle Ages down to Hanoverian times, for it served the corn crop on which this country depended, quite literally, for its daily bread.

The standardised pattern of this type of building was determined centuries ago by the storage and processing needs of the grain harvest. In its simplest form, it consisted of two end bays separated by a central passage served by two pairs of double doors in opposite walls and fitted with a hard floor. At harvest time, waggons came into the barn from the fields through one door, unloaded their sheaves and left by the other door. Then, in the winter, these sheaves were taken down from the dark ends of the barn and thrashed by flail on the central floor. Finally the grain was winnowed by being tossed in the air by either a wooden shovel or a scoop-shaped basket called a winnowing-fan, the chaff being carried away in the through draught created by pinning open both sets of doors.

Large barns had two passages, two thrashing floors and two sets of doors. Large farms had two barns, one for the

A 'cruck' barn in Herefordshire, probably built in the later Middle Ages. A 'cruck' was made of long, heavy timbers cut from naturally curving trees, roughly squared, split in two and set opposite each other, either in the earth or on a stone base, to make the arches which formed the framework of the building.

A new use for an old barn. A Tudor barn en route to a new site in the grounds of Knebworth House, Hertfordshire, where it now serves as a restaurant.

wheat which was sold off the farm, one for the oats and barley which were used on it. But all barns on all farms were built on the same principles and all fulfilled the same functions.

Most of the barns that stand on farms today probably date from the seventeenth and eighteenth centuries. But they include some of the few medieval farm buildings that survive. These are the huge and gracious barns commonly, but sometimes wrongly, called tithe barns. The name is correctly given to those which were built on ecclesiastical estates to store tithes, a form of tax paid to the Church not in money but in kind, mostly corn, though the name is sometimes casually used to cover all old barns. The largest of these magnificent buildings, which was 303 feet long and 54 feet wide and covered nearly a third of an acre, no longer exists. But others almost as large can be seen to this day. One fourteenth century barn was still in use twenty-five years ago, when it housed two tractors, feedingstuffs, fer-

tilisers, hay and straw, an eight-stall stable and pens for a hundred pigs. It served, in fact, as a farmstead on its own.

In the nineteenth century the mechanisation of thrashing, the purpose around which the barn was designed, brought at first rapid change and then sudden obsolescence. The early thrashing machines, which were usually driven by four-legged horse power but occasionally by water-power, could commonly be fitted with little difficulty into the traditional type of barn. By the 1820s such machines were common, so common that many were attacked and destroyed by the labourers whom they deprived of precious winter work.

In 1827 a special Act of Parliament was passed to protect the machines by imposing heavy penalties on those who damaged them. Then, in early Victorian times, the new and mighty power of steam came to the farm and began to replace the horse and the waterwheel even as they had replaced

Thrashing by flail in the late 18th century, seen inside the barn. The 'basket' on the left is a winnowing fan used for casting the grain into the air to separate it from the chaff in the draught provided by opening the doors of the barn. The thrashing floor was commonly of oak planks or a mixture of earth, clay and dung beaten until it was 'solid, hard and firm'.

the human flailer.

Soon the steam engine became normal equipment on the larger and more advanced arable farms and to this day some of the factory-type chimneys built to serve this new form of barn-power still stand on our farms. But 'the steam-driven barn' did not last long, for the convenience of taking the thrashing machine to the corn stacks instead of bringing all the corn to the barn encouraged the development of portable thrashing machines hauled and driven by steam engines. As the years passed, therefore, more corn was thrashed in the fields and there was less need for the barn. So no more barns were built and existing barns were gradually adapted to other purposes or allowed to degenerate into dignified dumps for anything that could not be more conveniently stored elsewhere.

In our own time, however, a few of these old barns have recovered part of their ancient purpose, for they house the complicated equipment needed for drying and storing the sudden mass of grain which the combine harvester delivers at harvest time. So part of the harvest routine has returned in new form to its old home.

ABOVE: *An early Victorian thrashing machine. Such gear could be fitted quite easily into existing barns but it rendered new barns of the traditional size and design unnecessary.*

BELOW: *A 20th-century grain-dryer stands in a 19th-century barn where the flailers once worked. The tractor fuel store on the right also bears witness to the development of agricultural mechanisation.*

ABOVE: *The wheel of a Northumberland wheelhouse, also called a gin-gang. This wheel was turned by a horse and the power was transferred by a shaft to the thrashing machine in the adjacent barn. This gin-gang was built, probably in the early 19th century, of local stone and has been converted to house calves with the aid of concrete blocks.*

BELOW: *Another gin-gang in Northumberland. Compare this gin-gang built by local men from* local materials with the Dutch barn on the right, which consists of factory-made components brought to the farm and erected there.

FACING PAGE: *New forms of power come to the farmstead. On the left is the gin-gang, the circular house for the four-legged horse-power which drove the thrashing machine in the early 19th century. In early Victorian times animal power was replaced by the new and mighty power of steam.*

ABOVE: *The Great Barn built in 1791 by Wyatt for Coke of Norfolk, the famous 'improver' on his Holkham estate. Among other uses, it housed the exhibitions of livestock at his annual 'sheepshearings' when he kept open house for agriculturists.*

BELOW: *Part of the north range, including the barn, of a Staffordshire farmstead built in 1863. Here steam power was used for processing food for livestock which was distributed by trolleys running on a tramway. It also drove a sawmill.*

A granary of the type widespread in southern England by the 18th century. This one was built in 1731 and can be seen at the Weald and Downland Museum in West Sussex.

THE GRANARY

The thrashed grain required safe storage, for it was both the farmer's main cash crop and the seed for his future corn crops. Some farmers stored it in the barn or, better, in a room above the cartshed, where it was safe from damp. But many preferred to build a special granary which could be conveniently supervised and kept locked. These small rectangular buildings normally rested on four mushroom-shaped stands called staddle stones, which provided protection from rats and mice.

Nowadays these granaries are seldom used for their original purpose. The combine harvester and the complicated grain drying and storage equipment it entails has rendered them obsolete. But many remain on modern farms, contrasting pleasantly with the concrete and asbestos buildings around them, because the farmer finds them safe and useful stores for seeds, fertilisers, tools or spare parts.

ABOVE: *This combined granary and cartshed was built on a Worcestershire farm between 1770 and 1800 and now stands in the Avoncroft Museum of Buildings. When not housed in a separate granary, grain was commonly kept over the cartshed. The farmer had to store his grain off the ground to protect it from vermin and he could not store it over livestock buildings because of the danger of contamination. Note the dog kennels below the stairs. Corn was valuable and needed protection against thieves.*

FACING PAGE: *A typical granary, standing on staddle-stones which provide protection from rats and mice. This granary dates from Tudor times and was presented by the Marquis of Bath to the Lackham College of Agriculture. The photograph shows it being re-erected on the new site.*

CARTSHEDS AND IMPLEMENT SHEDS

Carts and waggons are substantial and expensive pieces of farm equipment. So it has always been worth the farmer's while to house them in, for example, open-sided lean-to sheds to protect them from the sun and rain which warp and rot their timberwork. Such shelters also probably housed the most important of the simple field implements of the time, for it was not until the early nineteenth century that there was much need to provide them with special accommodation.

As field machinery became more complicated, however, the need for better and larger implement housing increased. This process began with the drill in later Hanoverian times and has continued via the Victorian reaper-and-binder to the tractors and combine harvesters of today. So give the unpretentious implement shed more than a passing glance. Its size and its contents will tell you a good deal about the mechanisation of agriculture and the changes it has brought to the farm.

ABOVE: *A cattle shelter of unknown date in the Cotswolds. The pillars are said to have come from a nearby Roman villa. This simple type of shelter is common in yards all over the country, but many of the older ones have been demolished or replaced.*

FACING PAGE, TOP: *A 17th-century cowhouse in Derbyshire, partly modernised. The timber came from local forests, the cement for the concrete floor from distant factories.*

FACING PAGE, BOTTOM: *A traditional type of West Country cattleyard, with overhead 'tallet' for storing hay.*

CATTLE BUILDINGS

Cattle have always been important in the British farming system. They thrive on the grass for which our soil and climate are peculiarly suited and they produce meat and milk, leather and manure. Until mid-Victorian times, too, they also provided a great deal of the mobile power on which the farmer depended for the cultivation of his fields.

But their historical importance is not reflected by the older cattle buildings that have survived. For one thing, many cattle spent much of their time in the winter months not in buildings but in open yards, where they trod straw litter into manure. For another, many of the older cattle buildings were no more than shelters which later collapsed or were demolished. The shelter in a yard shown

above survived because it was built of stone. It might not have survived if it had been built of timber. Further, the more elaborate cattle buildings were those where the dairy herds were housed in winter and milked all the year round. Some of these old cowhouses have been adapted to meet the ever-increasing demands of hygiene and convenience in milk production. But most of them have been replaced either by improved types of cowhouse or by the more recently developed systems of parlours in which cows are milked and yards in which they are wintered. The development of milk production buildings is therefore better shown by historical illustrations than by surviving examples.

In the agricultural depression which began in the 1880s, milk production became increasingly important, since liquid milk was the only type of farm produce which did not face competition from overseas. Many farmers modernised old cowhouses. In the one shown above, the new concrete floor contrasts with the old stone walls. Some wealthy landowners, however, built new cowhouses, as shown below. In its day, half a century ago, this was a model for all to admire. Now it, too, is part of farming history.

In the days before the railways, people in London and other big cities relied for their milk on dairy herds housed in cowhouses in streets and squares. Here is one of these urban cowhouses in Regency times.

THE URBAN COWHOUSE

One unexpected type of cattle building has now disappeared completely. These are the urban cowhouses in the streets and squares of London and other great cities which, in the days before railways, provided townsmen with the milk they could not obtain from dairy farms.

Regency London, for instance, contained some 8,500 cows which spent their lives tethered in stalls from which they were let out into yards for water and exercise for a few hours a day. In general, sanitary conditions among these 'wretched beasts housed in dark shade and hovels, standing ankle deep in filth' were indescribably bad. So was the quality of their milk by the time it reached the customer. In Glasgow, it is true, William Harley showed that good housing and good management could produce good milk in the middle of an industrial city, but it was long before his standards became normal practice.

By the 1860s, however, reforms of the London cowhouses had produced 'such patterns of neatness and convenience' as Mr. Drewell's establishment in Upper Weymouth Street, Marylebone, which included a quarantine room for newly arrived cows, and Mr. Veale's 'clean, dry, warm and airy' cowshed in Acacia Road, St. John's Wood. But the days of even the best urban cowhouses were numbered. One by one, as

the system of milk trains developed and sanitary legislation intensified, they closed down. But the end was slow in coming. There were a thousand cows in Inner London, including a herd of 85 head in Bermondsey, as late as the 1930s and it was not until 1953 that the last cow was milked in the last cowhouse in the City of London.

TOP: *We think of concrete as a new material, but it was used on farms in mid-Victorian times. The building on the right is the first concrete farm building erected in Britain. This highly unusual cattle shed dates from 1870 and was built by an enterprising industrialist who owned an estate in Berkshire.*

RIGHT: *The corners of this mid-Victorian Scottish farmstead were carefully rounded to prevent passing stock injuring themselves on sharp corners.*

A model dairy built in 1870 by the Duke of Hamilton for the home farm of his Suffolk estate. The doors and windows are fitted with stained glass, many of the panels incorporating parts of the family arms, the shelves are marble, the walls tiled with birds and floral designs in white on a pale blue background and the tiled floor also includes coats of arms. The fountain is for cooling the room. Milk was churned into butter in the adjacent churn room and worked, weighed and wrapped in this dairy, some for the hall, some for the estate workers. An ornate dairy like this would not, of course, be found on any normal commercial farm, but it illustrates the survival of the aristocratic tradition in Victorian times. This building is now on view at Easton Farm Park in Suffolk.

THE FARMHOUSE DAIRY

Evil communications corrupt good manners. They also render impossible the general transport and sale of such a perishable commodity as milk. Until the coming of the railways, therefore, milk was processed on the farm into butter or cheese. This task was the responsibility of the farmer's wife and daughters whose workshops were rooms in the farmhouse, where milkroom, churning room, cheeseroom and storeroom might easily take up a substantial part of the ground floor.

The importance of these farm dairies is illustrated by the fiscal concessions granted to them by an Act of Parliament of 1795 which exempted their windows from Window Tax provided the word 'Dairy' or 'Cheeseroom' was inscribed over them 'in large roman letters of two inches at least in height and of proportionate width'. A few of these inscriptions survive, but the dairies themselves are now usually normal farmhouse rooms. When the trade in liquid milk developed, the old dairies to which milk was laboriously carried in pails across yards were replaced by new dairies adjacent to the cowhouse and convenient for the lorries which took the churns to the depot.

ABOVE LEFT: *The main wheel for horse-driven butter-making equipment in an advanced farm dairy of the late 18th or early 19th century.*

ABOVE RIGHT: *In the days before railways, when milk could only leave the farm as butter or cheese, cheese-presses of this traditional type* *were part of the equipment of many farm dairies.*

BELOW: *In the 19th century, methods and equipment became more sophisticated. Today farm cheese-making only survives on a few farms which have developed highly specialised forms of manufacture.*

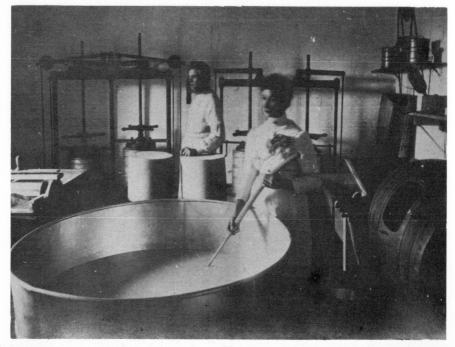

ABOVE: *The Victorian farm depended on literal horse-power, so good stabling was important. This mid-Victorian stable on a Staffordshire farm secured good ventilation by omitting a loft and providing louvred outlets at the ridge.*
BELOW: *A stable range on a Hampshire farm built in 1838. The horses lived on the ground floor and hay and straw were stored overhead.*

THE STABLE

Until the coming of the tractor in the present century, the stable housed the animal teams on which the farmer depended for the cultivation of his land and the haulage of his crops. Today, of course, we associate stables solely with horses. But for many centuries the farmer used oxen as well as horses as work beasts and it was only in Victorian times that the horned plough team became first a rarity and finally a curiosity.

Today the ox teams are forgotten and the horse teams are no more than a memory picturesquely revived from time to time by enthusiasts at local shows and ploughing matches. The stables have gone with them. Nothing is now left of the ox-stables except a few wide doors in some old Welsh buildings which recall the wide spread of the horns of the local breed of plough-ox. And little is left of the stalls that housed the horses that only two generations ago numbered over a million. Some have been demolished, others have been converted, often beyond the point of recognition, to other purposes.

An example of the traditional cottager's pigsty with a covered section for shelter and an open run which contained the food trough. This Staffordshire piggery was probably built in mid-Victorian times.

THE PIGGERY

The piggery is, rather surprisingly, a comparatively recent invention. For many centuries the domesticated pig, like its wild ancestors, was mainly a woodland animal, and in Saxon and medieval times pigs spent much of the year under the supervision of the village swineherd in the forests, where they foraged on beechnuts and acorns, grubs and carrion. The Normans who compiled Doomsday Book assessed the value of woodlands in terms of the number of pigs they could support. It was not until the seventeenth and eighteenth centuries that the conversion of the ancient forests to farmland compelled pigs to seek the permanent hospitality of the farmstead. In some areas piggeries were still regarded as an innovation in the early nineteenth century.

Sometimes pigs were housed in yards, but more commonly they lived in some version of the familiar cottager's pigsty which provides an open run and a warm shelter, a type of building peculiarly suitable for the pig which, being hairless, is more susceptible to climate than other farm animals.

On dairy farms, where pigs were fattened on the by-products of butter-making and cheesemaking in the farm dairy, there were often rows of such sties. On other farms, there were one or two sties near the farmhouse, where the farmer's wife could conveniently feed them on household waste. In the villages, too, many cottagers kept a pig or two in a sty in the back garden. This was, indeed, their main source of meat, sometimes their only source, and the pig was an important member of the village community. Readers of *Lark Rise to Candleford* by Flora Thompson, which gives such an unforgettable picture of life in an Oxfordshire hamlet in later Victorian and Edwardian times, will remember her description of the family pig as 'everybody's pride and everybody's business'. 'Callers on Sunday afternoon', she continues, 'came to see not the family but the pig and would lounge with its owner against the piggery door, scratching piggy's back and praising his points or turning up their noses in criticism.'

Nowadays, however, such sties are little used. On the farms they proved too expensive in labour and have been replaced by larger, more intensive types of piggery. In the villages their numbers decreased as sanitary standards improved. But when you see a derelict pigsty, remember that you are looking at a relic of the days when butter and cheese were made on farms and the countryman fattened, killed and ate his own pork and bacon.

ABOVE: *The pig was originally a woodland animal and herds of pigs foraged for themselves in the forests under the care of swineherds until the shrinking of the forests brought about the keeping of pigs at the farmstead. These 17th-century pigs, housed in a simple yard, preserve the long legs and lean bodies of their semi-wild ancestors.*

LEFT: *Wattle-and-daub, a common form of wall construction for buildings on farms from Saxon to Hanoverian times. Woven willow or hazel rods were formed into a sort of wickerwork and smeared with clay which filled up all the chinks and hardened as it dried.*

LEFT: *This steading is probably between 150 and 200 years old and therefore dates from the last age of rural sufficiency. The dovecote preserves the memory of the days when pigeons provided fresh meat in wintertime as well as valuable manure.*

RIGHT: *Internal view of a medieval dovecote, showing the revolving ladder from which the nests could be reached.*

A dovecote in Bedfordshire which was built in the first half of the 16th century. It is more elaborate and elegant than most such houses.

THE DOVECOTE

Nowadays we do not regard pigeons as a form of farm stock. But in the past their agricultural importance was considerable. They provided fresh meat and eggs to vary the limited diet of the times and they left valuable residues for the dunghill. In feudal times, however, these benefits were the monopoly of the lord of the manor. Only he could build the massive stone dove-towers of the early Normans or the lighter, more ornamental structures of their successors from which fluttered the winged flocks whose ceaseless depredations on neighbouring crops are remembered in the old rural proverb of the four grains sown in a row,

One for the pigeon, one for the crow,
One to rot and one to grow.
The order is significant.

As farming developed, the importance of pigeons decreased and men began to emphasise the harm they did to crops rather than the value of their meat and manure. The tradition died slowly. Some early nineteenth century farmers built lofts for doves in their barns or over their cartsheds and as late as the 1880s pigeons 'played a quite appreciable part in the economy of most farms' in Northamptonshire. But it is now a long time since domesticated pigeons have contributed more than pleasure and interest to the farm.

The oasthouse is the typical and delightful building of the hop-growing areas, but historically it is quite a recent development. Oasts of this type did not become common until the early 19th century. The men are holding 'pokes', the traditional bags in which hops were measured before being taken for drying.

THE OASTHOUSE

Hops were first cultivated in this country in Tudor times and with the hop garden came, inevitably, the oasthouse for drying the crop. But the early oasthouses were very different from those we now associate with the Kentish landscape. The familiar circular oast topped by a pivoted timber cowl with a flyboard to keep the back of the cowl to the wind did not become an established feature of the hop growing countryside until the early nineteenth century. It was invented in the 1790s, along with a garden syringe, a stomach-pump and a steam heating system for glasshouses, by

an ingenious gardener, John Read of Horsmonden, near Lamberhurst.

Farmers still use these oasts, but they no longer build them: the pre-war innovations of electric fans, oil-firing and roof louvres have combined to produce a more efficient though less artistic type of drying installation. So the mechanisation of drying this crop has rendered obsolete the traditional oasthouse even as the mechanisation of harvesting it has rendered obsolete the traditional annual migration of hop-pickers from London's East End.

A Somerset farmstead. Probably none of the buildings is less than a century old, but it is difficult to tell the age of farm buildings when traditional materials were used and traditional designs followed, as they changed so little over the generations.

THE FARMSTEAD FITTED TOGETHER

So far we have looked only at particular types of building. But, of course, each particular building is only one part of the whole farmstead. And the way in which a farmstead is planned and the different buildings are fitted together to form a practical and convenient pattern may well tell us as much about the farms and farmers of the past as the individual buildings which compose it.

Men have built farmsteads ever since they first began to cultivate the soil, and one type of farmstead can trace its ancestry back to Neolithic times. This is the longhouse, which shelters the farmer's family and his livestock all under one roof: some have survived to our own time. But the basic plan of most of the farmsteads that we see today dates from the period 1750 to 1880. For

this there are two reasons. Firstly, this was a period of great agricultural development and expansion. It began with the Agricultural Revolution of George III's time and ended with the prosperous and progressive High Farming of mid-Victorian times. Consequently, in these years many old farmsteads were reconstructed and many new ones built to meet the needs of the new farming systems. Secondly, in the later eighteenth century the leaders of the farming industry evolved a highly standardised and effective type of farmstead design which, with a multitude of local modifications and variations, was copied all over the country and was continued by their nineteenth century successors.

This standard-pattern farmstead was designed to meet the needs of the farmer who both grew crops and kept stock in the mixed farming system which was, and still is, predominant in this country. On the one hand, this farmstead provided accommodation for his corn crops and the means of accumulating the manure to maintain the fertility of the fields that grew them. On the other, it provided convenient housing for his varied livestock.

Essentially, this type of farmstead consisted of three parts. The first was the barn, in which corn from the stackyard was thrashed and from which straw was distributed. The second was the collection of livestock buildings in which hay and straw were processed into manure. The third was the yard formed by the barn and livestock buildings, where stock exercised and manure accumulated.

Such farmsteads took the form of a series of buildings round open yards, occasionally in a square, more commonly on three sides of a square, some with one yard forming a U-pattern, some with two yards forming an E-pattern. The yards faced south to catch the sun and to avoid some of the rainy south-west winds. They were sheltered on the north by the barn, the largest building on the farm—the hiker today can still often orient himself by the position of a barn in a farmstead—and by the cartsheds which usually faced north to avoid sun and rain. From this north range and at right angles to it ran the wings which enclosed the yard and contained a medley of buildings, some for storage, most of them for livestock, the stables commonly facing east to catch the rising sun which literally lightened the early morning labours of the carter and ploughman. Pigs were usually housed near the farmhouse since they depended on the by-products of the dairy and the household, as did the poultry which were traditionally the concern of the farmer's wife. Convenient to the cattle buildings, sometimes in a barn, sometimes in stacks, stood the haystore. The farmhouse, normally on the south of the farmstead, completed this agricultural factory.

The Hanoverians were dependent on local materials for their buildings. Except in a few areas served by the new canals, they used timber from local woods, stone from local quarries, clay from local pits, thatch from local fields, bricks and tiles from local kilns. In Hampshire, for instance, even the tar came as a by-product from the local manufacturer of gunpowder. The Victorians, living in the age of railways and factories, could use brick, tiles and slates produced in any part of the country. They could obtain such new materials as asphalt, creosote and, more important, cheap glass for windows, and they could also buy such prefabricated equipment as ventilation cowls, guttering, mangers and cast iron pillars and trusses. Further, they could instal steam power, whereas their fathers depended on the labour of men and animals. At first sight, therefore, their farmsteads look very different from those of their fathers.

But only at first sight. It is soon clear that the Victorian farmstead is essentially an industrialised version of the Hanoverian farmstead. It is built with industrially produced materials and fitted with industrially produced equipment, but it serves similar needs in a similar way. In particular, it continues the old pattern of north range and south-facing yards.

The later nineteenth century saw the beginning of a long period of agricultural depression which lasted to the 1930s, when few new buildings and fewer new farmsteads were erected. Since then, however, there has been a great deal of new construction with, inevitably, the destruction of many old buildings. So today there are few wholly Hanoverian or wholly Victorian farmsteads, although some include older buildings and nearly all include later buildings, adaptations or alterations. In many cases the original pattern, preserved either by the original buildings or by their successors, is still visible and it is possible to trace the basic plan prepared a century, a century and a half or two centuries ago, and to appreciate the principles and traditions that went to its making.

30

FURTHER READING

Brigden, R. *Victorian Farms.* Crowood Press, 1986.
Brunskill, R. W. *Traditional Farm Buildings of Britain.* Gollancz, 1982.
Darley, G. *The National Trust Book of the Farm.* National Trust and Weidenfeld & Nicholson, 1981.
Fenton, A., and Walker, B. *The Rural Architecture of Scotland.* John Donald, 1981.
Fowler, P. *Farms in England.* Royal Commission on Historical Monuments, 1983.
Harris, Richard. *Discovering Timber-framed Buildings.* Shire Publications, 1978.
Harvey, N. *A History of Farm Buildings in England and Wales.* David and Charles, 2nd edition, 1984.
Horn, W., and Born, E. *The Barns of Beaulieu and its Granges at Great Coxwell and Beaulieu St Leonards.* Berkeley, Los Angeles, USA, 1965.
Hughes, G. *Barns of Rural Britain.* Herbert Press, 1985.
Martin, D., and Martin, B. *Old Farm Buildings in Eastern Sussex, 1450-1750.* The Rape of Hastings Architectural Survey, The Flat, 16 Langham Road, Robertsbridge, Sussex, 1982.
Morton, R. S. *Traditional Farm Architecture in Scotland.* Ramsey Head Press, 1976.
Peters, J. E. C. *Discovering Traditional Farm Buildings.* Shire Publications, 1981.
Peters, J. E. C. *The Development of Farm Buildings in Western Lowland Staffordshire up to 1900.* Manchester University Press, 1969.
Robinson, J. M. *Georgian Model Farms.* Oxford University Press, 1983.
SPAB Barns Book. Society for the Protection of Ancient Buildings, 1982.
Wade-Martins, S. *A Great Estate at Work.* Cambridge University Press, 1980.
Weller, J. *History of the Farmstead. Development of Energy Sources.* Faber, 1982.
Wiliam, E. *Traditional Farm Buildings in North-east Wales, 1550-1900.* Welsh Folk Museum, 1982.
Wiliam, E. *The Historical Farm Buildings of Wales.* John Donald, 1986.
Woodforde, J. *Farm Buildings.* Routledge & Kegan Paul, 1983.

SOURCES OF INFORMATION

Historic Farm Buildings Study: Farm Buildings Group, Land and Water Service, Ministry of Agriculture, Fisheries and Food, Great Westminster House, Horseferry Road, London SW1, 1986. A comprehensive reference source on old farm buildings in England and Wales. It includes a bibliography, information on numbers and types of existing old farm buildings, and a list of such buildings open to the public.
A Bibliography of Vernacular Architecture by R. de Z. Hall, David and Charles, 1982, and *A Current Bibliograph of Vernacular Architecture, 1960-76 by D. J. H. Michelmore.,* Vernacular Architecture Group, 1979, which supplements it, contain sections listing books and articles on old farm buildings.

PLACES TO VISIT

In recent years there has been a remarkable increase in the number of agricultural museums and farm parks. A few are specially concerned with buildings, including farm buildings, but many also use them to house other exhibits. Examples of regional and local centres are given below. Your county museum will be able to advise you on farm museums and buildings of interest in your area. Intending visitors are advised to ascertain times of opening before making a special journey.
Acton Scott Working Farm Museum, Wenlock Lodge, Acton Scott, Church Stretton, Shropshire. Telephone: Marshbrook (06946) 306.
Avoncroft Museum of Buildings, Stoke Heath, Bromsgrove, Worcestershire. Telephone: Bromsgrove (0527) 31363.
Chiltern Open Air Museum, Newland Park, Gorelands Lane, Chalfont St Giles, Buckinghamshire. Telephone: Chalfont St Giles (02407) 7117.

Cogges Agricultural Heritage Museum, Church Lane, Cogges, Witney, Oxfordshire. Telephone: Witney (0993) 72602.

Easton Farm Park, Model Farm, Easton, Woodbridge, Suffolk. Telephone: Wickham Market (0728) 746475.

Elvaston Working Estate Museum, Elvaston Castle, Elvaston, Derby DE7 3EP. Telephone: Derby (0332) 73799.

The Great Barn, Avebury, Marlborough, Wiltshire SN8 1RF. Telephone: Avebury (067 23) 333.

The Great Barn, Great Coxwell, Faringdon, Oxfordshire.

Hampshire Farm Museum, Manor Farm, Upper Hamble Country Park, Botley, Hampshire. Telephone: Botley (04892) 6304.

Highland Folk Museum, Duke Street, Kingussie, Inverness-shire PH21 1JG. Telephone: Kingussie (05402) 307.

Lackham Agricultural Museum, Lackham College of Agriculture, Lacock, Wiltshire. Telephone: Chippenham (0249) 656111.

Model Farm Collection, Wolvesnewton, Chepstow, Gwent. Telephone: Wolvesnewton (029 15) 231.

Museum of East Anglian Life, Abbots Hall, Stowmarket, Suffolk IP14 1DP. Telephone: Stowmarket (044 92) 2229.

Museum of Kent Rural Life, Cobtree Manor Park, Lock Lane, Sandling, Maidstone, Kent ME14 3AU. Telephone: Maidstone (0622) 63936.

North of England Open Air Museum, Beamish Hall, Stanley, County Durham. DH9 0RG. Telephone: Stanley (0207) 31811.

Pitstone Green Farm Museum, Pitstone, Buckinghamshire. Telephone: Cheddington (0296) 668223.

Ryedale Folk Museum, Hutton le Hole, York YO6 6UA. Telephone: Lastingham (075 15) 367.

Shugborough Farm Park, Shugborough, Staffordshire. Telephone: Little Haywood (0889) 881388.

Tatton Park, Knutsford, Cheshire. Telephone: Knutsford (0565) 54822.

Weald and Downland Open Air Museum, Singleton, Chichester, West Sussex. Telephone: Singleton (024 363) 348.

Welsh Folk Museum, St Fagans, Cardiff, South Glamorgan CF5 6XB. Telephone: Cardiff (0222) 569441.

Wimpole Home Farm, Arrington, Royston, Hertfordshire SG8 0BW. Telephone: Cambridge (0223) 207257.

Wye College Agricultural Museum, Brook, Ashford, Kent TN24 5AH. Telephone: Wye (0233) 812401.

ACKNOWLEDGEMENTS
Illustrations are acknowledged as follows: Ancroft Museum of Buildings, page 15; F. Cottrill, Winchester City Museums, page 23 (bottom); East Lothian County Council County Planning Committee, pages 11, 20 (bottom); *Farmers Weekly*, pages 4 (bottom), 9 (bottom), 16 (bottom), 26 (bottom); John Gray, page 20 (top); J. A. Hellen, page 10 (both); J. M. Kerr, Easton Farm Park, page 21; Lackham College of Agriculture, page 14; Cadbury Lamb, pages 13, 27 and front cover; Mimram Studio, page 7; National Dairy Council, page 19; J. E. C. Peters, pages 12 (bottom), 23 (top), 24; North of England Open Air Museum, Beamish, page 31; John Read, page 29; Edwin Smith, pages 16 (top), 17; University of Reading Museum of English Rural Life, pages 1, 2, 3, 5, 8, 9 (top), 12 (top), 18 (both), 22 (all), 25 (both), 26 (top), 28; David Uttley, page 4 (top); Weald and Downland Open Air Museum, Singleton, page 13; R. Winstone ARPS, page 6.